The stars fall in.
Over my right shoulder,
they whisper Psalms of my ancestors.
I listen.
On my ladder.
Under the crescent moon.
Illuminated.
I write.

CONVERSATIONS
IN A
MIRROR
ON A
LADDER

BEAUTIFULLY, POETICALLY CRAFTED BY

Rob Naylor Jr.

FIRST VOLUME

CONVERSATIONS IN A MIRROR ON A LADDER
Copyright © 2018 by Rob Naylor Jr.

ISBN 978-0-578-20265-5
Printed in USA

In loving memory of my mom, Beverly Ann (Jackson) Naylor.

ACKNOWLEDGMENTS.

Support systems and acknowledgments of appreciation are priceless. I want to thank each and every person individually, but there are not enough pages available. Having said that, if I do not mention your name, please blame it on the page restriction and not my heart. I dedicate this book to my mom, Beverly Ann (Jackson) Naylor. It never gets easier to accept that you are no longer here, but I speak to your spirit daily.

I appreciate my parents (Robert L. Naylor Sr. and Pam M. Naylor) beyond words for guiding me in the right direction and instilling the values in me that make me the man that I am today. It was a rough road, but we made it. Thank you to my little super heroes aka my kids (Malachi, Amari, Jordyn and Kayvon-Legend) for always reminding me that I am unbreakable.

A very special thank you goes to my wife for always being my biggest cheerleader and vital source of help in completing this project as well as in life. To all of my siblings (Sherry, Necie, Helen, and Atlas), I love you past the moon and back. We may not talk every day, and we may be geographically separated, but we remain close. I appreciate any and everyone who has ever had a hand in helping me learn a lesson no matter how big or small.

Thank you to Rod Cannon (Photo credit: Me on the ladder/front & back cover) who took time out of his hectic schedule to pencil me in for a last minute photo-shoot. Finally I want to thank you for taking the time to read this book. You being inspired by my words inspires me. I truly appreciate you. As cliche as it may sound, if I can inspire just one person, I can rest easy as I slowly move through the other side of the hour glass. Love.

CONTENTS...

MORE CONTENTS...

PREFACE

This is not (just) a poetry book. It is not your colloquial collection of contemporary prose. This is relatable, authentic, introspective creative therapy authored to heal, and inspire us. On Christmas Eve of 1990, my mom went to the hospital. At 8 years old, I had no idea that was the last time I would ever see her. When she died, I disappeared.

I went "somewhere else" I went "nowhere". Twenty-seven years and countless blocked memories later, I still find myself listening for the doorbell, hoping it's her finger that pressed the button. I have always been one to compartmentalize my emotions, but conversations in the mirror have helped me climb the ladder; from "nowhere". Life is good, but it has a mean undertone. Through photography as well as the art of creative writing, I share my thoughts and experiences on death, divorcing religion, racism, prejudice, doubt, self-worth, mental health and love.

Conversations in a Mirror on a Ladder is a daily good-read.

I wrote this for generations past, present and future. Equipped with inspiration and affirmations, this editorial experience was beautifully crafted to foster the spiritual and mental resiliency needed to help us climb the ladder.

She stares.

With caliginous eyes, she quietly storms.
Her passive aggressive tone is inviting.
Her crimson dress undulating in the wind.

As she dances into the night,
I am tempted to follow.

I forego her advances.

Feet firmly planted,
I sit and take a moment to reflect.
I lift my head toward the clouds.

The ladder disappears into uncertainty.

I climb to escape the turbulence,
but not without us.

CROSSING.

Death is awful.
The carousel keeps spinning and it's impossible to get off.
Nine thousand eight hundred fifty-five days ago, I flatlined.
Time of death,twelve twenty-four
After two thousand nine hundred seventy-four days
on this earth,
I was inducted into a brotherhood.
A not so secret,
secret society.
A painful probate.
My heart crossed.
Hazing at its worst.

I died.

The twenty-fourth day of December for me
is eternally marked with crimson "X".
Continuous REM,
my gift as I lie consciously unconscious
"somewhere else".
"Nowhere at all".

No safety belt as I accelerate in the DeLorean.
Perpetual pain floods my temporal lobe.
Paralyzed.

Condolences are but energy on the shore line, recording as I
grasp for traction.
Gasping for air.

Empathy is my life preserver.
Time is my lifeguard.

"BETA BETA TAU".
BROTHERS BONDED BY TRAGEDY.

Brother,
I can relate.
I also lost my mother.
When I heard your angel spread her wings
my mended heart broke.

We are more alike than different.
I see you hurting. I feel your pain.
Scabs peel.
I bleed for you.
I do not say much because I know words do not
"fix it".

Condolences are appreciated, but they spend
like an "IOU".
Although you may feel alone, you are in good
company.

Alone in good company.
A brotherhood of broken hearts.
Shattered.
Together.

A fraternity of brothers bonded by tragedy.

ARMY OF ONE.

We stand as one.
Together.

Occasionally glancing over our left shoulder.
She seductively dances to the rhythm of our heartbeat.
Her crimson dress flowing like aggressive waves
ripping through the ocean.

Together we stand.
Free.
Fetters on feet.
Roots buried in quicksand.
History lost.
Still searching for the treasure map.

3yes right!
Glimmers of light periodically manifest.
Hearts remain broken.
Together.

Never alone.
Alone, but together.
We stand as one.

Feet firmly planted.

We survived a series of inescapable moments.

Moments authored by an omnipotent hand.

I'm not famous.

So the mention of my name is not trending on your timeline.
I'm not famous so I hope my words still
find their way to your spirit.

I don't have a million followers on any social media platform.
So I stand firm.
In touch with foundations laid before me.

No viral videos.

Just medicinal belles-lettres pre-scribed for healing via my pen.

I don't want to be famous, but I desire my gems to shine on
red carpets as they dance under the light of the crescent moon.

I am confident beyond measure, yet find myself

constantly trying to measure up.

I am an introverted extrovert

Lonely in the crowd.

Candid conversations on the ladder

keep me grounded.

My grandmother once told me

masturbation makes Jesus cry.

So, I remain humble.

DOUBT.

What if...

The man I desire to be and who I am destined to become never meet?

Success often feels closer than it appears.

Here,
I am an outsider.

An introverted extrovert.

In the company of intimate circles,
I am a triangle.

Lost.

Inconsistently searching for an entrance.

Consistently.

A triangle in the company of small circles.

SILENT SCREAMING TREE.

In the middle of a crowd, there is nobody around.

When I fall, I still make a sound.

My aura can be easily misconstrued.

Misunderstood.

My serene outward appearance is often a misrepresentation of the storm inside.

Tranquil during turbulent storms.

Nobody hears me.

Silent screams unnoticed; ignored in the middle of the forrest.

Listen closely and you can hear me silently scream...

when I fall.

"DO NOT ALLOW
YOURSELF TO BE DEFINED
BY ANYONE
OR ANY ONE THING".

My first love…

My identity.

My sanctuary.

I can still smell her aroma.

Therapy.

My escape.

Still close, but I fear we have grown apart.
Familiar strangers.

We rarely converse, but I see her often.
Enjoying life with new versions of me.
I was her muse.

I sit lonely in a crowded gym.

I watch her.

I sit patiently awaiting acknowledgment.

We used to spend every day together.
Now we only see each other in passing.

Priorities change direction without warning.

As time passes, so do we.
My love for her will never...

FADE AWAY.

THE ARTIST'S CREED.

I am an artist.

My heart does not march to the cadence
of popularity.

My purpose is deeper.

My venue is for V.I.P only.
I do not wish to sell out.

Popularity is temporary.

I do not craft excellence for pictures.
I create to immortalize my genius.

Over and again.

When my flesh returns to dirt,
I will turn to sand.

Falling through the hour glass.

Edifying.
Inspiring.
Living...

Forever.

Letting go is a valuable learned skill.

It is vital to survival.

A prerequisite to climbing the ladder.

Letting go comes with wisdom.

Lessons from the old owl.

Survival requires a solid support system.

Someone to talk to.

Counseling is...
Taboo.
It's for weak minds.
We don't do that.
We are not crazy.
It won't work.

Counseling is...
Acceptable.
It's for strong minds.
We need it.
We are not crazy.
 It works.

Life is a team effort.

AFFIRMATIONS.

You are a meticulously crafted masterpiece.

An aesthetically pleasing, beautiful hue.

Painted by perfection.

The picture they forge from falshood
is stroked with ignorance.

Never purchase their depiction of you.

Their direction is flawed.

CONFIDENCE.

I am a forty thousand, three hundred twenty-one-piece puzzle personified.

Shattered.

 Resilient.

  Confident.

"THERE IS WISDOM
IN EVERY SCAR.
EVERY SCAR
HAS A STORY".

SCARS.

Perception is that you do not
belong here.
Realistically, you are precisely
where you need to be.
I remember it like yesterday.
Father Time had taken
the day off.

Sound survival advice ignored.

In a hurry to go nowhere,
I slipped.

Gravity imposed her will.

I was swiftly lifted from my
death bed.

Not all heroes wear capes.

Blood on the walls as my
consciousness slowly faded.

Time stood still.

Right hand in left palm.
Left thumb tucked
underneath the right one.

My father's wisdom manifest.
A permanent fixture.

Light in times of darkness.
Guiding my sailboat to safety.

His cautionary sentiments
affixed above my left brow.
An aesthetically boisterous,
silent reminder that he is with me
forever.

Guiding my vessel to safety.

DIFFERENT.

I am different.

I am not wired the same.

Different is where I am comfortable.

It is not what I am.

It is who I am.

GUILTY.

I am guilty.

In blood diamond chains.

I traverse stolen,
blood soaked soil.

Free.

Truthfully,
I feel I have the power to change the
world.

Actually,
I see this is an ambitious notion,
a lofty venture dipped in black gold.

What makes you so special?

Life cycles and priorities change.

The carousel keeps spinning.

A powerful wavering tone dominates the sky

and echoes into the night.

It plays on a loop for about

three to five minutes at a time.

Attack in progress.

There is an internal battle within

and a war going on outside.

A war that not one of us are safe from.

BEYOND THE BRUSH.

Forgive me.

Or don't.

I am not in search of, nor do I long for your forgiveness.

This is my journey.

I wrap my soul in Egyptian Cotton and create my bindle.

The stars as my guide, I journey toward the crescent moon.

My soul wonders.

Exploring.

Lost.

Searching for peace.

There is discernment beyond the brush.

SAIL.

My peace of mind
would not allow me
to continue to
journey with you.

No grudges
harbored.

Anchor lifted.

Ship sailed.

Kwaheri.

Research expanded
my world view.

When I was a child,
I walked down the
aisle.

Baptized.

Drenched in
indoctrination.

Unaware of the
commitment required
of this union.

Tradition is no reason to
jump the broom.

Letting go was difficult.
Life started when I left
you.

It was an arduous but
necessary decision.

No more safety net.

No anchor.

Sail.

DOCKED.

I took a leap of faith and landed in a river.

The levee broke.
River waters rushed.

Evolution ensued.

Today,
as I walk through the valley of the
shadow of death,
I find comfort in
tomorrow.

I find solace in understanding that God
works for me within my very own mind.

When I tell people you and I are no longer
together, they assume I am with her.

I admit,

I see her often.

With caliginous eyes she stares.
Dancing to the rhythm of my heartbeat.
Her crimson dress flows like the ocean waves.

Tempted, I forgo her advances.

Logic over emotion.

Empathy over apathy.

Love over libation.

I took a leap of faith and drowned in the river.

Righteousness flows through me

in the midst of the battle.

Setting sail was difficult.

Without a safety net, I became more aware.

I put my headphones on to lift my spirit.
For four minutes and fourteen seconds,
the noise faded away.
"I'm the man, I'm the man, I'm the man".

The fabric of our society was
woven by
perpetual prejudice.
Stitched with genuine generational
antipathy for my personage.

I stand and fight for the good.
He knelt for justice.
For us.

America's kitchen is filthy and
in dire need of a deep cleaning,
but it is not my responsibility to sweep.

The onus of change is on the ones who
soiled the floors, but we have the power to
rearrange our cabinet.

I have the power to change.
We have the power to create change.

So, there I was...
Surrounded.
Black cloud looming.

Enemy fire rains.
Bullets barely miss me.
They whisper as they pass.

Not guilty, but I fit the description.
Male, black, 3'0" to 8'1".
Age three to ninety-nine.
Under International Humanitarian Law
and the Geneva Conventions,
religious buildings are offered special
protection.

So why are we purposely
slain in perpetuity?

Rules of engagement clearly, merely a suggestion.

Eleven pleas discharged.

I watch from above.

Reminded of my short stay at the
Algiers.

My weapon lay motionless.
Flat on the concrete, empty.

BREATHLESS.

PSYCHOLOGY.

America...
The beautifully ugly Gemini.

Illusions of invincibility rule.
No exceptions.
3yes wide open while theirs are wide shut.

Fear is kin to caution.
IT lies dormant,
hibernating.
Penny-wise.
Awaiting seasons change.

Confusion transitions to understanding.
Moments of clarity.
I cautiously journey the road
frequently traveled.

Flashing lights ~~haunt~~ hunt my psyche,
demanding I pull over,
No sudden movements.
They feed on our fear.
The future of my kingdom,
my legacy
hinges upon my ability to navigate
blood-soaked terrain with no map.

Survival is the objective.

Always armed.
Melanin is my weapon.
Knowledge my ammunition.

They used to hide in the woods.
Underneath hoods.
Now they show face in red brim.

Only in their own six by nine do they yield
significance.

Sadly,

We still allow them to call the shots.

It's time to ghost their power.

Pull back the blinds,

we've reached the crescendo.

Change by any means in my right hand,

MALCOLM IN THE WINDOW.

To survive in this black mirror,
I must remember my lines and act accordingly
I must stick to the script.
(Police) lights,
(body) camera,
action!

The land of the free…
with exception.

A counterproductive system,
backward in direction.

Home of the brave.

Built for free, by the hands of slave.

Confinement under the guise of freedom.

Indoctrination is standard operating procedure.

I carry my weapon through foreign land fueled by selfish
selfless promise.

A country indivisible, united in division.

Who is mine enemy?

Tears of my ancestors fill ducts, but refuse to fall.

Existing in a war zone is disturbingly, comfortably
uncomfortably…

"HOME".

"I am the coolest monkey
in the jungle"?
How many generations
and ways are you going to
shoot us in a hoodie,
in the dark,
in the light?

The trump card turned hope to hopelessness.
A penny with a whole in it.

Delusions of grandeur unfiltered.

Skeletons of yesterday unearthed.

Dirty kitchens and messy cabinets exposed.

How should we handle this?
How do we survive here?

History is made while
HIStory is
repeating, repeating, repeating,
repeating, repeating, repeating
repeating, repeating, repeating,
repeating, repeating, repeating
repeating, repeating, repeating,
repeating, repeating,
repeating...

THE SPIRIT OF 68'.

When wisdom speaks, we must listen.
I had the honor, privilege and pleasure of interviewing
Dr. John W. Carlos for *"The Black Power"* issue of
Empire Radio Magazine.

Myself and my good friend and (super)photographer
Ricky LeBaron Godette were invited to Atlanta to conduct the
interview. Little did we know, Mr. Carlos had much more in
store than just an interview. We were invited to a dinner at his
good friend Mel Pender's beautiful home. Mel Pender is a
decorated Vietnam war combat veteran. He served in the U.S.
Army for 21 years and retired at the rank of Captain in 1976.
He and I exchanged stories about the military and differences
between the Air Force and Army. Of course there were the
colloquial jokes about how "easy" the Air Force is in contrast to
the Army.

We heard all of his military and track and field stories as
he took us on a trip down memory lane and a tour of what I call
his "room of accomplishments and awards". It was everything I
envisioned my basement to look like, but much larger.

Mr. Pender is also the winner of a gold medal in the
4x100 m relay at the 1968 Summer Olympics. I got to see the
medal in its museum like casing first hand along with the track
spikes dipped in gold.

We also met other polarizing athletes of the day all of
whom are good friends with Dr. Carlos and Mr. Pender. Their
competitive nature still burns as bright as the day the match was
lit as they told stories of the days they were in their prime.

Dr. Carlos' stories were captivating. As we sat in the backyard partaking of the delicious assortment of pulled pork, chicken, and all of the other foods that are making me hungry as I type this, everyone listened as he told a chapter book of stories. Hilarious stories. One story he told was about a chicken he had brought home when he was a kid growing up in New York. You have to grab his book "The John Carlos Story" for more insight on his pet chicken, but to hear it in person was priceless.

After dinner, Dr. Carlos, Ricky and I found a quiet room in the house and set up for a candid conversation. That day, we learned much more than what Dr. Carlos taught us about life. We learned that we have to be more prepared with our equipment. Ricky's camera battery died and we were left with figuring out how to improvise. Hence the Facebook live footage via my iPhone. Although the video quality is not what I had hoped for, Dr. Carlos' words covered all bases. His message was perfectly conveyed. If you take time to listen and see beyond the visual aesthetics (or lack thereof) you will be inspired.

I am forever thankful for the opportunity to reach into his brain.

One of the gems he gave us that really stuck with me was when he said, *"You're the one [who is] supposed to be orchestrating how you set up your cabinet"...*

What I took from that powerful statement is that I, you, we have the power to create change.

The stories and insight Dr. Carlos shared with me over the phone prior to the trip to Atlanta were very deep, insightful and life changing. One day I will share them. Just not today.

EGG SHELLS.

I am a man.

Chin up.

I journey through decades of treacherous terrain
layered with soot covered egg shells.
Egg shells tossed from windows of the kitchen
in the house where I was born.

Blood still on the floor.
Not enough fingers lifted to mop it up.

Dirt swept under the rug.

A kitchen with prearranged expired contents
inside dark cabinets.
Dark closets crowded with bones and fossils.

In my raised, clinched fist lies power.
The power to orchestrate how I set up my cabinet.
I open the third floor window.

The pungent odor of burned temples lingers.

The smoke has yet to dissipate.

I am a man.
My keen optics is well aware that your eyes are wide shut.
Illuminated or not, police lights in my rear-view
cause palpitations.
Perspiration bathes my steering wheel.
Life flashes.

I am a man.
Naked.
Brutally beaten beyond recognition.
Fastened to a 75-pound cotton gin fan with barbed wire.
Tossed into the Tallahatchie River.
I gasp for air.

Consciousness restored.

The bright lights from a well-lit Soundview vestibule is safe.
I am safe.

This is home.

Suddenly 41 bullets burn through my anatomy.
The lights burn brighter.
I walk into them.

I am a man.

Generations lost.
Buried under rivers my ancestors drowned in.
Gems extracted from aquifers.
Bullets fly, ropes hang and shackles abound.
We have been victorious in many battles, but the war rages on.

I am a man.

(AD)VANTAGE POINT.

A tree with too many branches to
accurately count stands tall in the middle of the sea.

Violent waves systematically destroy
precious branches.

Over time,
some are broken, some are bent,
some are bruised.
Some are undamaged.

Watching the tree safely from the white sand on the
shore, one can assume nothing is wrong.

All they see is branches.

To them they all look the same.
Undamaged.

If only they would make the effort to swim.
If only they would make the effort to take a closer look.

Empathy, due diligence.

Comfortable, willful ignorance.

#WORD2HANCOCK

The closer we get to one another,

the more human we become.

Ironically you make me superhuman.

I travel through infinite lifetimes to find you.

Until I do.

DÉJÀ VU...

TRAVELERS.

Foundations of an omnipresent heart.
Solid and fragile.

Eternal internal energy existing.
Circulating outside of our consciousness.

Souls intertwined.
Ignoring the hands dancing around the clock,
only to discover foundations reminiscent of another time.

Bedraggled, resilient hearts beat.
Dark clouds loiter overhead.
Existing in the moment.
Living outside of our comprehension.
Comfortably restless.
Lying atop baggage scattered inside of a glass house.
Absolute uncertainty tapping on windows.

We've met before.

Together always despite storms.
Auspicious stars eclipse crossed celestial bodies.
Our hearts murmur in unison as we traverse the universe.
Oblivious to its laws.
Passers by,
travelers in a familiar, foreign time.

Déjà vu written in cursive on a broken pendulum.
Bound by expectation.
Destined to meet an ambiguous end, a constant fate.
Inevitably, helplessly, hopelessly,
souls mate.

LOVE IS A UFO. LOVE IS A UNICORN. LOVE IS SASQUACH.
LOVE IS A MYTHICAL THING WE ARE ALL IN SEARCH OF.
LOVE IS SPECIAL.
FIND LOVE.
CAPTURE LOVE.
CHERISH LOVE.
LOVE LOVE.
ALL LOVE.
ONE
LOVE.

Funny story...

This one time this "thing"
happened to me.
Once upon a time,
I caught a catfish.

I was on a sailboat
searching for peace.

I longed for calm waters after a
beautiful storm.
I glanced port side.
There she was, walking on the
surface of
calm seas.
She stared.

With caliginous eyes s
he quietly stormed.
Her passive
aggressive tone was inviting.
Seductive.

She danced to Sirens song.

I joined her.

Her crimson dress was
flowing in sync with the
ocean waves.

A beautiful dark twisted
fantasy.

I was Blindly
tangled in the web.
F%@k tradition!
Third finger to caution.

Violent currents triumph.
Vessel capsized.
Trapped in a premonition
that never came to fruition.
Enamored with
the idea of you.

Truth hidden in plain sight,
but I turn a blind 3ye.
Lost in the triangle.

I was completely
submerged in the aesthetics
that lie in shallow waters.

When I came up for air,
I realized,
you were never here.

CATFISH.

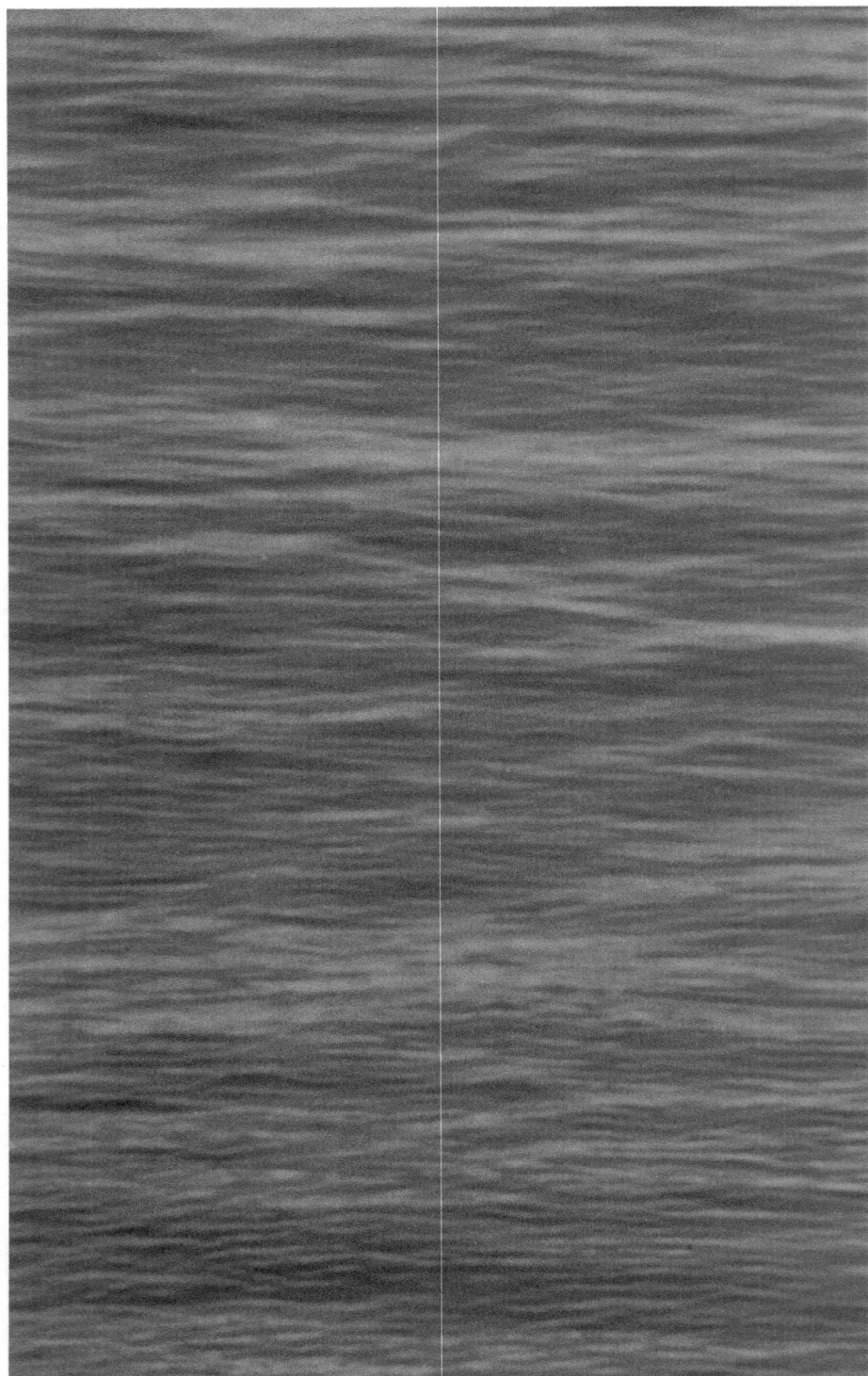

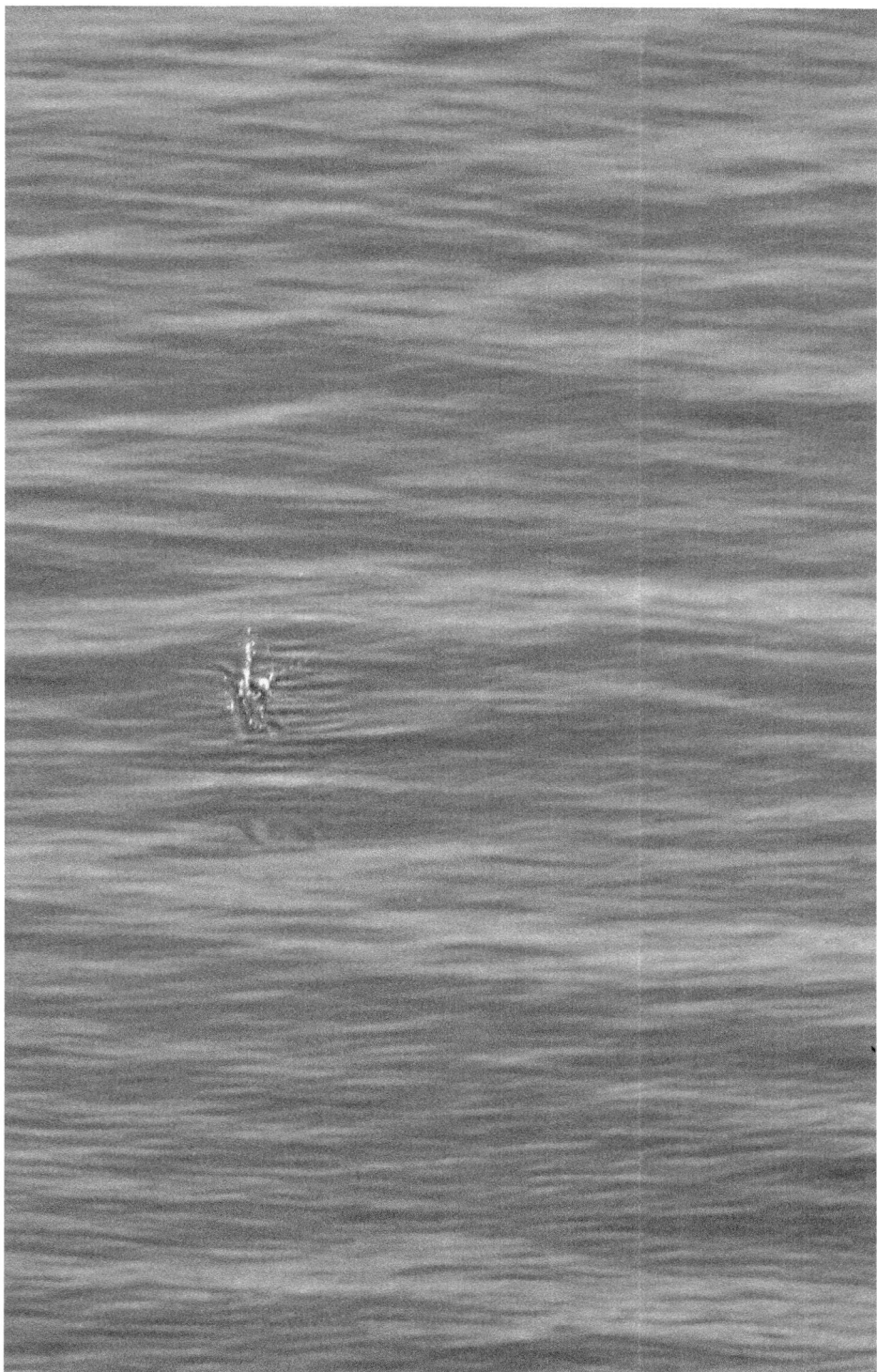

DESTINATION NOWHERE.

Speeding through life is a waste of time.
I used to be in a hurry.
I used to speed.
In a rush to nowhere.

Like, at the grocery store, or driving in my big ass Impala
I was always in such a hurry.
I am intrigued by people age fifty five or greater.
I was going to say "elderly", but after a quick Google search,
apparently elderly is derogatory.
So, I am intrigued by people age fifty five or greater.
AARP eligible...or whatever.
That probably sounds weird without context.

I'll explain.

I am enamored with wisdom.

With each day that passes, I take however many steps my
Apple watch tracks toward the end of this life.
Steps toward wisdom,
steps to the beach chair,
but at the same time,
they are steps to nowhere.

People age fifty five or greater have so much wisdom.
So much experience.

I watch as society burns in the microwave.

As we pass by one another, our greetings are
typically so quick, we don't even stop to hear the
answer to "how are you doing?".

I can just imagine all that they have had the
opportunity to witness in their long life.
Pillars of knowledge with the cheat code to life.

While I am on fast forward flying through the
parking lot at the grocery store trying to find the
closest parking spot, Usain Bolt[ing] through the aisles like
I was running in the Olympics or determined to win on an
episode of *Supermarket Sweep*.

Or switching lane to lane
going 90 miles per hour on Highway 64.

They drive slowly.

Meticulous in their motions, they gingerly glide through life.
They slowly maneuver through aisles careful to not miss a
thing on their shopping list.

In my haste, I always forget something.
I get home and realize I forgot to get eggs, or milk or
something I knew I should have gotten, but didn't
because I was in a rush.

Speeding through life is a waste of time.

RECEIPT.

Time is a precious gift.
Throw away the receipt.

Live, laugh, love.

Embrace compassion.
Give no energy to hate.
Time is precious.

Life is a gift.

You only get one and there is a
no return policy.
It's yours.

Enjoy life.
Live, laugh, love.
Throw away the receipt.

Aging beats the alternative.

Life is short, but ironically
life is the longest thing
you will ever do.

Life is a journey.

A road trip.

Enjoy the scenic route.

EMBRACE AGE.

SOBER HIGH THOUGHTS

In life, we are taught that there is a natural order.
We live and then we die.
From the starting line, we are newborn, then nurtured
into a toddler.
Then come our adolescent years where we then run full
speed through the wall into our teenage years.
And then reality hits when we are tossed into the ocean
of adulthood.

We are taught that adulthood is the last stop.
Adulthood is where the bus unloads.
But what if there is more?
Another stop.

What if death is not the end.
What if it is the beginning?
A trap door to a new stage where we play a new role?

One of the toughest things in life is to accept that we
do not know as much as we think we know.
To think that we are smarter than we actually are is one
of our most dangerous flaws.
It is tough to sway our minds in the direction that
allows us to admit that.

We don't have all the answers.

We are often of the mindset that anything outside of
our realm of comprehension is alien.

A black mirror never to be gazed into.
A deep, dark abyss never to be explored.

We struggle through life and rely on comfortable
stained glass safety nets to catch us when we fall.

Life is a game of emotional tug of war between
good and evil. God and D'evil.

No grey area.
But what if there is a grey area?

What if we are tangled in grey's anatomy?
A prerequisite to something else
A gateway leading somewhere else…

The ladder stops.

I look down to see how far I have come.

There she was.

Staring.

With caliginous eyes she ~~quietly~~ storms.

Aggressive winds rock my foundation.

Her ~~passive~~ pugnacious tone is ~~inviting~~ demanding.

Urging me to come down.

As she dances below,

I ~~am tempted to~~ follow.

J.T.E.Z
[JOURNEY THROUGH THE EPIPELAGIC ZONE.]

I have been there.
The place where obscurity and clarity meet.
It's dark there.

The place where father time is benumbed.
2716.5 feet in the air I stood under the crescent moon.

sinking.

I glance over the edge.
Just as I prepare to jump, an owl appears.
Perched on the ledge.

He stares.
With Incandescent eyes, he quietly storms.

Bright light breaks through the darkness of velvet dark
clouds, into the windows of my soul.
The warmth of son shine revitalizes my spirit.

I am awake.

Inescapable moments authored by an omnipotent hand.
I lift my head toward the clouds
The ladder ~~disappears~~ appears.
Extending into uncertainty.
I climb to escape the turbulence.

But not without **us**.

OWL IN MY BACKYARD.

An owl lives in my back yard.
Perched,
motionless.

A conduit of wisdom.

He whispers to me daily.

He quietly speaks volumes
through illuminated windows.

The guardian of my garden.

He guides me through life.

YOU ARE A
DESCENDANT OF A
RESILIENT
PEOPLE.
SUCCESS IS RELATIVE.
GREATNESS
IS IN YOUR DNA.

To them you are the picture of perfection.
A superhero too good for a cape.
They don't see what you see.

A mere mortal lost with no map.
Searching for direction.

They do not see the confusion when you are
stuck at an intersection.

They are unaware of the tears that flow into
the river in the dark as you sit idol at the
crossroads.

To them you are super dad,
the picture of perfection.

The one to follow
when in need of direction.

See yourself as they do.

PERSPECTIVE.

"YOUR VESSEL IS GUIDED BY MOOR,

YOUR DESTINATION IS CERTAIN.

LET KNOWLEDGE BE YOUR LIGHTHOUSE.

STAY FOCUSED".

PERFECTION.

Perfection is a Farris wheel.

The top is a matter of perspective.

When you think you have made it,
the top moves.

The journey continues.

MOMMY.

I apologize for blaming you
for leaving, as if you packed your travel bags.

I apologize for being angry at you for not being here to
hug me when I hurt.

To give me a band-aid on my knee when I fell.

To place a band-aid on my heart when it broke.

For not being here to yell at me when my room is a mess.

For not being here to approve of each girl I dated.

For not being here to teach me how to treat them.

I apologize for being disappointed that you were not
here to hold your grandchildren when they were born.

To spoil them, and give them cookies and candy before
dinner.

I apologize for blaming you.

Now I sit here patiently waiting
to tell you face to face...
I apologize.

MA'S LEMONADE.

You did the best you could
with what you were given.

One of the worst lemons.

I was somewhere else.

Someone else.

Yet you still did your very best to mold me into
somebody;
to lead me somewhere,
from nowhere.

And you did.

Thank you for making lemonade.

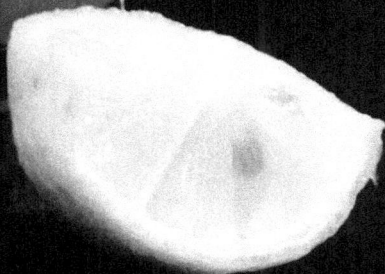

Cherish mom.
Never allow gravity to take hold of her crown.

The gift of her presence is to never be taken for granted.

Place her on the highest pedestal.

She may not be perfect, but she is...

Queen.

You may not understand her reasons.

Your best interest is her highest priority.

The terms and conditions of life do not allow for a replacement.

Take care of her.
Appreciate her.
Love her.

CROWN HER.

HINDSIGHT.

Chill...
You are doing a whole lot
for nothing.
Doing nothing will cost
you a whole lot.

I understand your anger.
I relate to your (lack of)
motivation.
Please understand that
your future is in your
hands.

Life is an ocean.
When you find yourself
sailing in open water,
storms will arise and
currents will pull you
under.

As the water reaches your
forehead,
you must make the
decision to swim to the
surface for air,
or drown.

There is a lighthouse in the
distance guiding you to
safety,
but that light cannot help
you unless you decide to
swim.

FORESIGHT.

The gym was my sanctuary.
~~#BallisLife~~ (Basket)Ball was life.
I developed an obsession.
A complex.
I was pressed to become the best.
I convinced myself that there was someone
who could see me working
and we wanted the same thing.
To be the best

Rain or shine I dribbled, I got shots up.
I ran laps, ran sprints, and ran suicides.
I could see him working on his game.
Trying to outwork me.
If I slept, he would work out and outwork me.
I got so caught up on his progress and forgot
about my own.

I lost focus on my growth.
What I learned is, not to measure
myself by my competition.
I am my own competition.
You are your own competition.
When you think you have worked hard,
work harder.

Do not measure your success by others.
Outwork hard work and
work hard.

Strive daily to become the best version of you.

I feel for you.

Prisoner to customs that
precede your existence.

An active participant in invariable
perpetual contradiction.

Guilty of your own demise.

Vices with the characteristics of vice grips.

Red cups at the alter.

Talent drowns in ambiguity.
Avant-garde composers whisper.

I hear them over the ambient light of acclaim.

I listen for you.
I feel you.
I feel for you.

POP CULTURE.

FEAR.

I only fear two things.

Success and reincarnation.

I don't fear failure because there is
no such thing.

What is considered to be failure is
a lesson learned.
An opportunity to grow, evolve,
fly, swim.

I do not fear death
because death is a part of life.
Energy transferred.

I fear dying and coming back as a
person who subscribes to failure.

I fear dying and coming back as a
person consumed by fear.

I fear three things.

ME ELEVATING ABOVE ALL THE NEGATIVITY. 💯

With every day that passes,
 I become more enamored with you.

I don't want to rush this.

I hate that I ever took you for granted.

I realize that at any moment,
I can lose you.

So I elevate above all negativity.

Carefully crafted masterpieces.*

Episodes directed by abecedarian Gods.

I am grateful to experience you daily.

Love

LIFE.

"PERCEPTION
VERSUS
REALITY
IS
THE DIFFERENCE
BETWEEN SURVIVAL
AND
BECOMING A
CASUALTY".

CLIMB...

ROB NAYLOR JR.
————— CREATIVE WRITER —————
SINCE 1992

www.ingramcontent.com/pod-product-compliance
Lightning Source LLC
Chambersburg PA
CBHW060950040426
42445CB00011B/1087